Who We Are

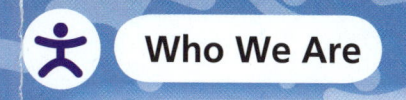

Our Bodies

Physical skills and attributes

Why do you think the boy in the story is called Big Barry Baker?

How are people's bodies different? How are they the same?

On a separate piece of paper, complete a Venn diagram for you and a friend, showing which of your physical features are similar and which are different.

Barry Baker loved cricket. List the parts of the body that are most important for playing cricket.

Give reasons for your answers.

_____

_____

_____

Liz had watched cricket on the television so she knew what to do. She walked away from Big Barry Baker. She stopped and turned, then she ran across the playground and bowled the ball.

12

All the children laughed.
'Big Barry Baker can't hit the ball,' they called out.
Barry was cross.
'I don't like cricket,' he said. 'I don't want to play.'
'You can't be good at everything first time,' said Liz. 'You need to keep trying.'
'I know,' said Roy. 'Let's go to the park after school. We can all have another go there.'

But Big Barry Baker missed.

So Liz bowled the ball again but not so fast.

Big Barry Baker missed again.

13

Learner Profile Attributes: Knowledgeable, Inquirers

1

Who We Are

Physical skills and attributes

Big Barry Baker was good at bowling and catching but not so good at batting.

Can you think of some other games that involve batting, catching or bowling?

Fill in the table.

Action	Game
batting	
catching	
bowling	

Which sports do you like? What are you good at?

Draw yourself doing one of these sports.

Learner Profile Attributes: Knowledgeable, Inquirers

Who We Are

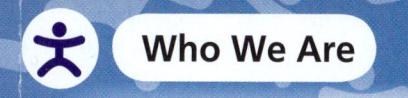

How important are these skills and attitudes?

Different games and sports need different skills and attributes, such as size, strength, stamina, speed, balance and accuracy. Use a dictionary to find out what these words mean.

Size: _____   Speed: _____

Strength: _____   Balance: _____

Stamina: _____   Accuracy: _____

Make a list of activities, games and sports, and show how important these skills and attributes are for your activities.

Use this key or make your own: V = very important S = somewhat important
N = not important

Activity	Size	Strength	Stamina	Speed	Balance	Accuracy
Cricket						

Learner Profile Attributes: Knowledgeable, Inquirers

Who We Are

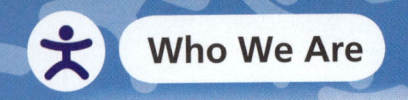

The skeletal and muscular system

The skills and attributes mentioned on the previous page depend on our skeletal and muscular system.

Our skeleton is made from lots of bones joined together. Bones are rigid.

Feel where your bones and joints are.

How many bones do you have? _____

How many joints do you have? _____

We move different parts of our body by using different muscles. Muscles are flexible.

Move different parts of your body. Can you feel your muscles? Where are they?

Find a large sheet of paper. Working with a partner, make a large paper outline of your body on the sheet. Now draw your skeleton. Show the bones and joints. Then add the muscles.

Learner Profile Attributes: Knowledgeable, Inquirers

Who We Are

The digestive system

Find out how different kinds of teeth work.

Incisors:

_____

Canines:

_____

Molars:

_____

Incisors

People have different types of teeth. They are called **incisors**, **canines**, and **molars**. All these teeth work in different ways to help us eat.

Teeth for eating

People need teeth for eating. We need to eat to stay alive and to grow. Our teeth break up food so we can swallow it.

What animals have these kinds of teeth?
Write the names of the animals into the correct categories in the table.

Animals that have incisors	Animals that have canines	Animals that have molars

Learner Profile Attributes: Knowledgeable, Inquirers

Who We Are

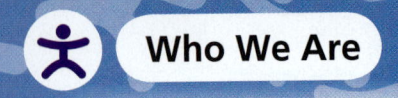

The stages of the human digestive system

Teeth are an important part of our digestive system. What happens when we first see, smell or think about food, before our teeth start working? What happens after we swallow our food? Complete the flow chart to show the main stages of the human digestive system.

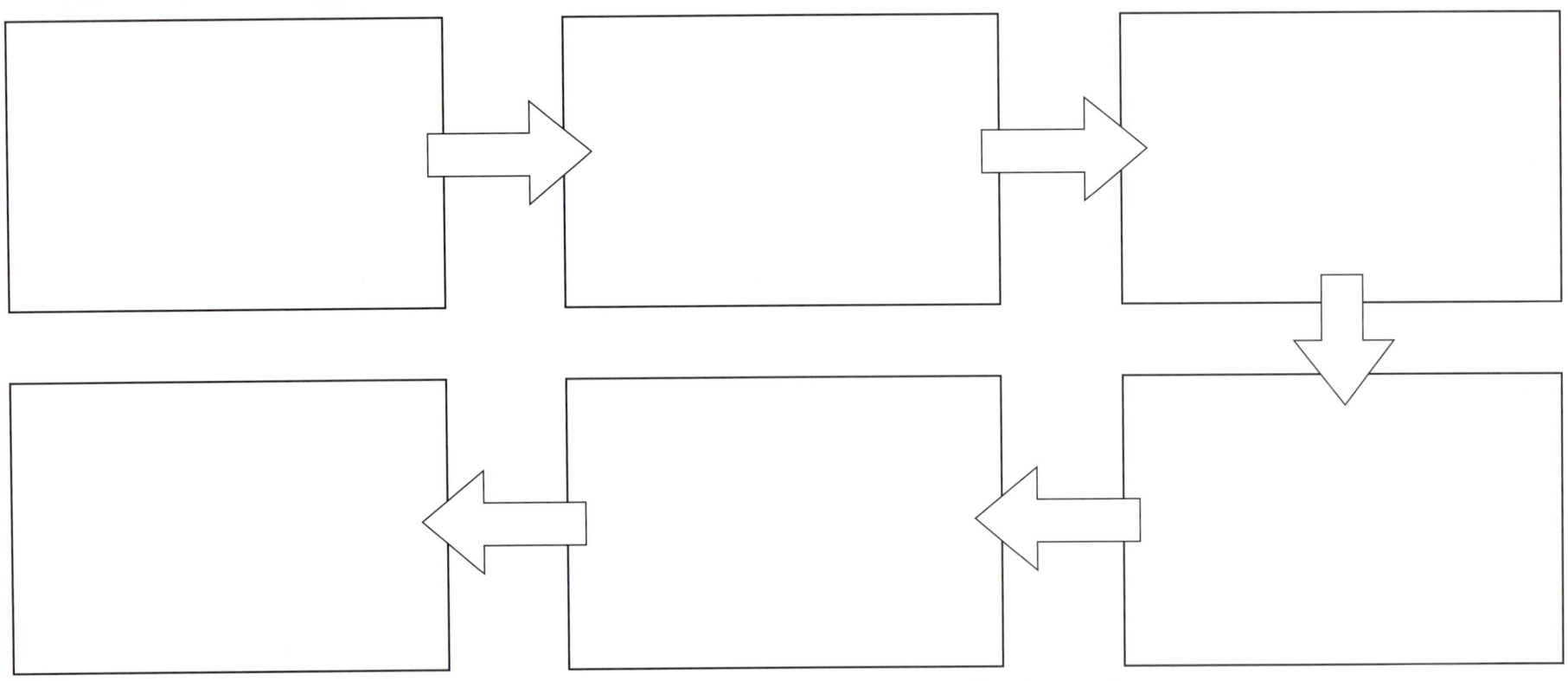

Not all digestive systems work in the same way. Find out how cows and other animals process their food.

Learner Profile Attributes: Knowledgeable, Inquirers

Who We Are

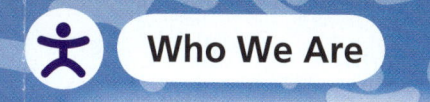

The brain and the nervous system

Our nervous system is controlled by the brain. It monitors and coordinates the other systems. Information from our senses (sight, hearing, touch, smell and taste) goes to the brain along the nerves. The brain processes the information (called a stimulus) and decides how to react.

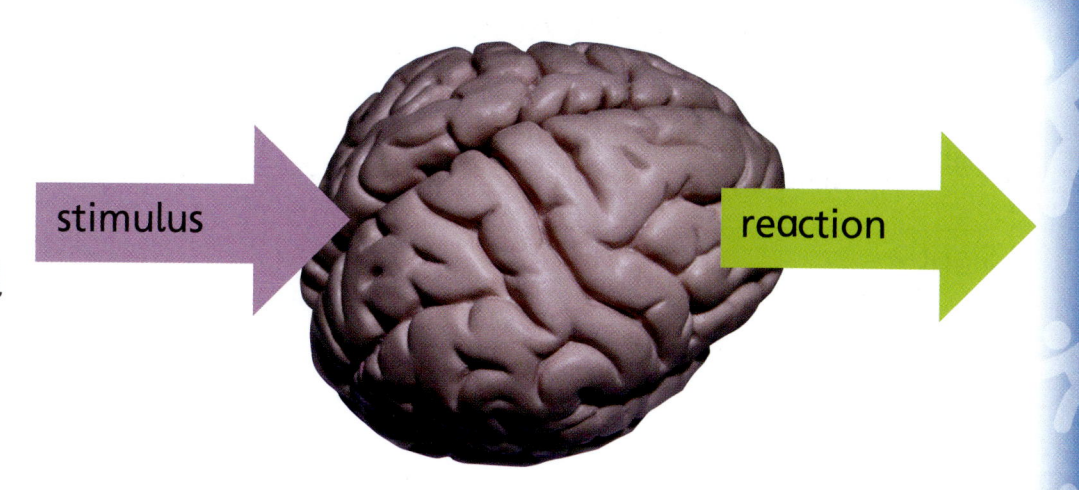

stimulus → reaction

Do some experiments to see how people react to different stimuli. Then complete the table on the next page. Use some of the ideas below or think of your own. The hearing, touch, smell and taste tests work best if they close their eyes or you blindfold them.

sight	hearing	touch	smell	taste
Possible stimuli: • a funny or scary picture • a kaleidoscope • an optical illusion	Possible stimuli: • a musical instrument • a sound sequence • a sudden noise	Possible stimuli: • different types of fabric • cold pasta or jelly and custard • ice cubes	Possible stimuli: • perfume • coffee • cut grass	Possible stimuli: • white/brown bread • different coloured fruit pastilles • lemon juice

Learner Profile Attributes: Knowledgeable, Inquirers

Who We Are

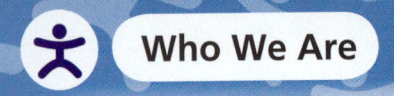

The brain and the nervous system

Sense	Stimulus	Reaction
Sight 1		Person 1:
		Person 2:
Sight 2		Person 1:
		Person 2:
Hearing 1		Person 1:
		Person 2:
Hearing 2		Person 1:
		Person 2:
Touch 1		Person 1:
		Person 2:
Touch 2		Person 1:
		Person 2:
Smell 1		Person 1:
		Person 2:
Smell 2		Person 1:
		Person 2:
Taste 1		Person 1:
		Person 2:
Taste 2		Person 1:
		Person 2:

⚠️ **Important safety note!** Never shine bright lights in eyes; never make loud noises close to ears; never use anything sharp or hot or otherwise dangerous.

Learner Profile Attributes: Knowledgeable, Inquirers

Who We Are

The respiration and circulation system

When we breathe we take air into our lungs. The lungs take in the oxygen we need, then they breathe out the unwanted carbon dioxide. This is our respiration system.

The oxygen goes into our blood and the heart pumps the blood around the body. This is our circulation system.

When we exercise, our lungs and heart need to work harder to take in more air and pump our blood more quickly. You can see this by measuring your heart rate. Get your friend to take your pulse after doing different types and amounts of exercise.

Activity	Heart beats per minute
sitting and reading quietly for 5 minutes	
hopping slowly on the spot for 20 seconds	
running fast round the playground or gym for 1 minute	

Learner Profile Attributes: Knowledgeable, Inquirers

Who We Are

The respiration and circulation system

Look at these words. Sort them into two categories: respiration or circulation. Then draw a diagram of each system and use the words to label the different parts.

arteries blood capillaries chest diaphragm heart lungs mouth nose oxygen throat veins	
Respiration system lungs	**Circulation system** heart
Diagram of the respiration system	Diagram of the circulation system

Learner Profile Attributes: Knowledgeable, Inquirers

Where We Are in Place and Time

Mapping

Place and time

On the map:

1. write the children's names next to their pictures and write the name of their country

2. draw an arrow to show the country where you are now, write your name next to it and draw a picture of yourself

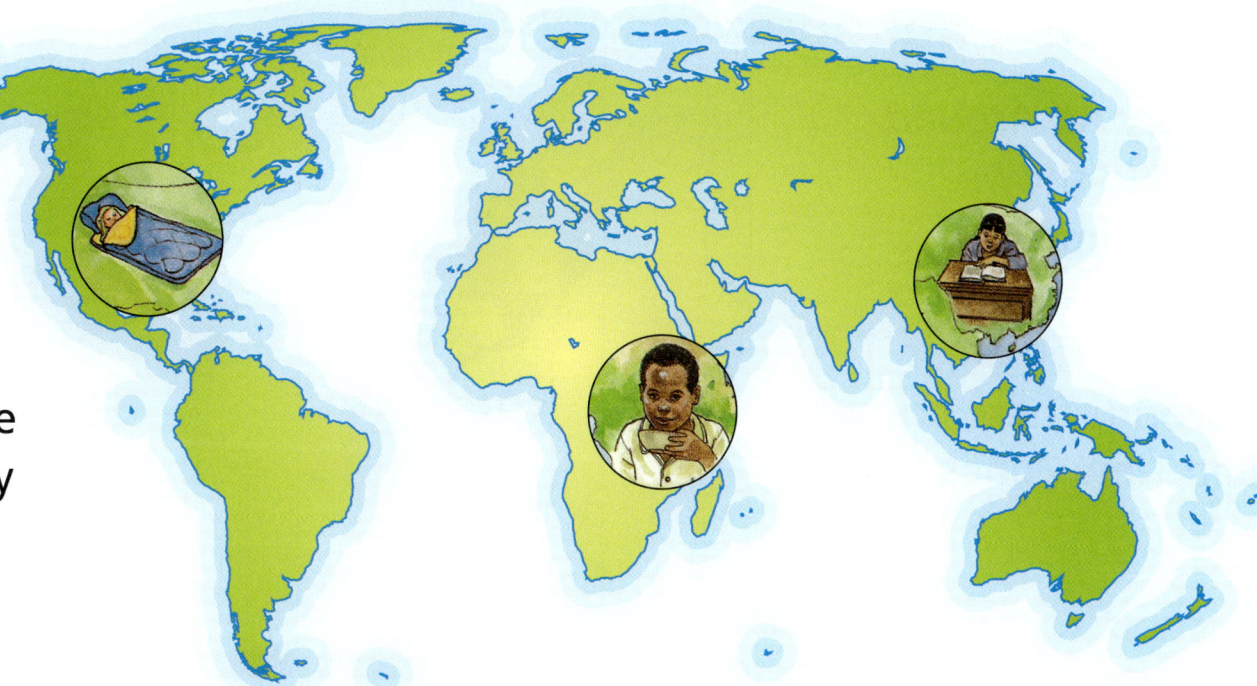

In America it is night and Sara is sleeping.
In Kenya it is morning and Kiprotich is eating his breakfast.
In China it is afternoon and Liping is sitting at her desk.

In Kenya it is morning, in China it is afternoon and in America it is night. All around the world children are eating, learning and sleeping – just like you!

3. write in the names of any other countries you know and draw a symbol if you have lived or been on holiday there, or if you have friends or family there (for example, draw a house symbol for countries you have lived in).

Learner Profile Attributes: Thinkers, Well-balanced

Where We Are in Place and Time

Time Zones

The story *All Around the World* shows that the time is different depending on where you are in the world. These are called **Time Zones**.

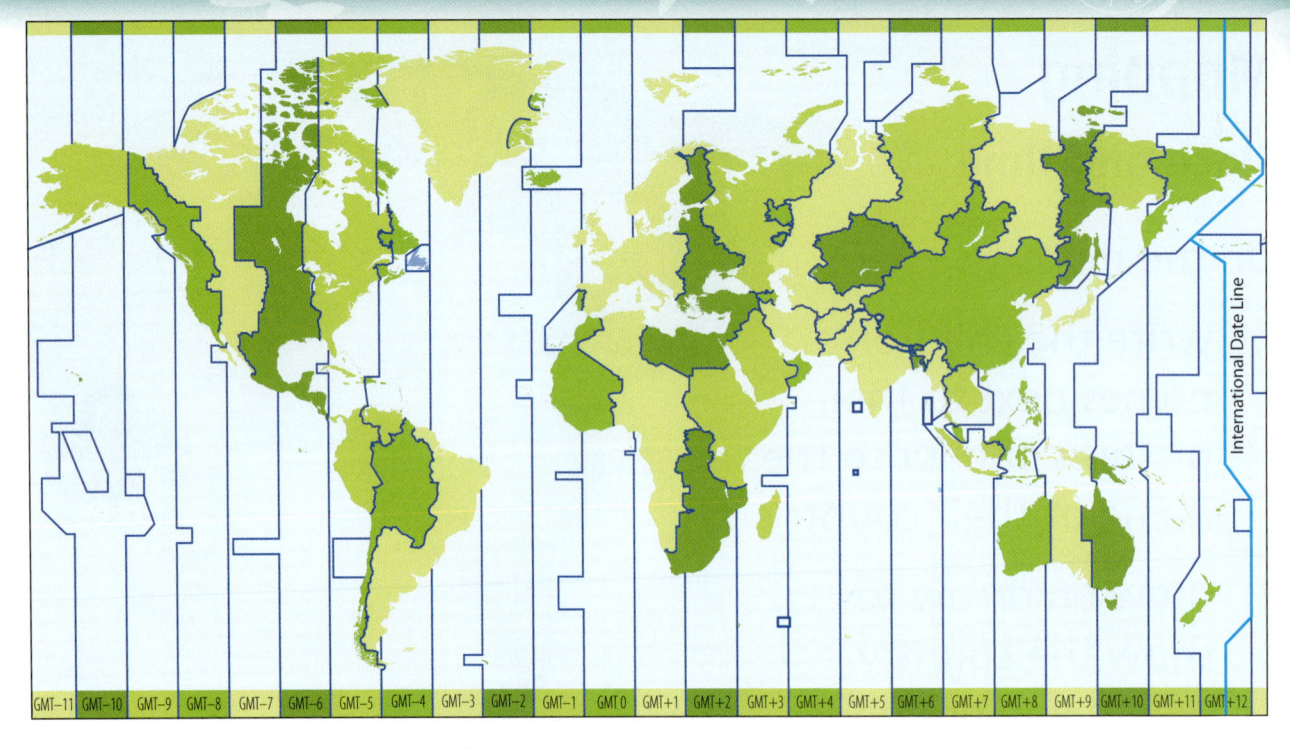

Complete the table to show the time now in different Time Zones.
Use digital times, e.g. 20:00 for 8 o'clock in the evening.

Who is where?	morning	afternoon	night
I am in _____.			
Sara is in America.			
Kiprotich is in Kenya.			
Liping is in China.			

Learner Profile Attributes: Thinkers, Well-balanced

Where We Are in Place and Time

Reading maps

Maps have many features that help you to read them.

Map title

Most maps have a **title**. A map title tells you what information is on the map. For example, a map of a small town may list the town's name as the map title.

Compass rose

Many maps have a **compass rose**. This feature shows the **cardinal directions**. The cardinal directions are north, south, east, and west. North often points towards the top of the map.

Look at the map of Milton town centre.

Where is the residential area in relation to the rest of the town? _____

Is the fire station to the north, south, east or west of the park? _____

Pick two locations on the map. Ask your friend for directions to get from one place to another.

Learner Profile Attributes: Thinkers, Well-balanced

Where We Are in Place and Time

Types of maps

Use the map on the previous page to complete these written directions:

The school is to the _____ of _____.

Oak Close is to the _____ of _____.

The fire station is to the _____ of _____.

Try giving verbal directions from one place to another using the words north, south, east and west.

Look in books, magazines and newspapers; in school, in the library and on the Internet. What types of maps are there and what do they show? Make a list.

Learner Profile Attributes: Thinkers, Well-balanced

Where We Are in Place and Time

Map symbols

Maps have many **symbols**. Symbols are small shapes and signs that represent objects in real life. For example, dots on a map may show cities. A star may show the **capital** of a country. The capital is the place where leaders of a country meet and work.

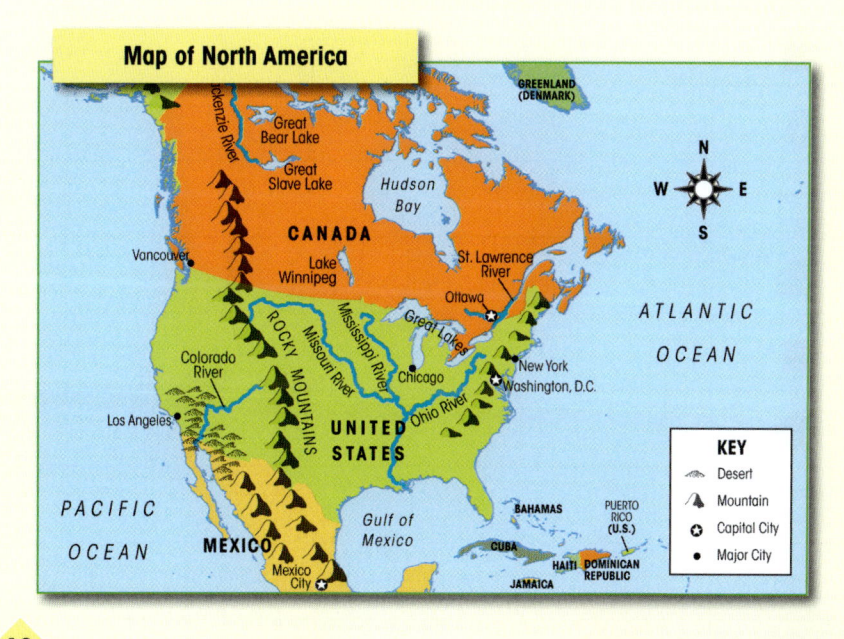

Map of North America

This map uses symbols to show where the main places and features are.

On a large sheet of paper, draw or trace an outline map of the country you live in.

Use colours and symbols to show the main places, such as the capital city and major cities, and features, if any, e.g. mountains and rivers.

Draw a key to show what they mean.

Add a compass rose to show direction.

Learner Profile Attributes: Thinkers, Well-balanced

Where We Are in Place and Time

Reading map symbols

Mapping your town or city

A map of a town or city shows an even larger area than a neighbourhood. It shows the location of important buildings, parks, and roads. The features on a town or city map are even smaller than the features on a neighbourhood map.

Look at the symbols used on the map.

Complete the table by writing the names of the buildings next to the correct symbols.

Then create some symbols of your own for different buildings.

Symbol	Building represented
✚	
🏠	
🛡	
✉	
▇	
■	
⛑	
📖	

Learner Profile Attributes: Thinkers, Well-balanced

Where We Are in Place and Time

A map of my community

This map shows how colours can be used to show different features and buildings.

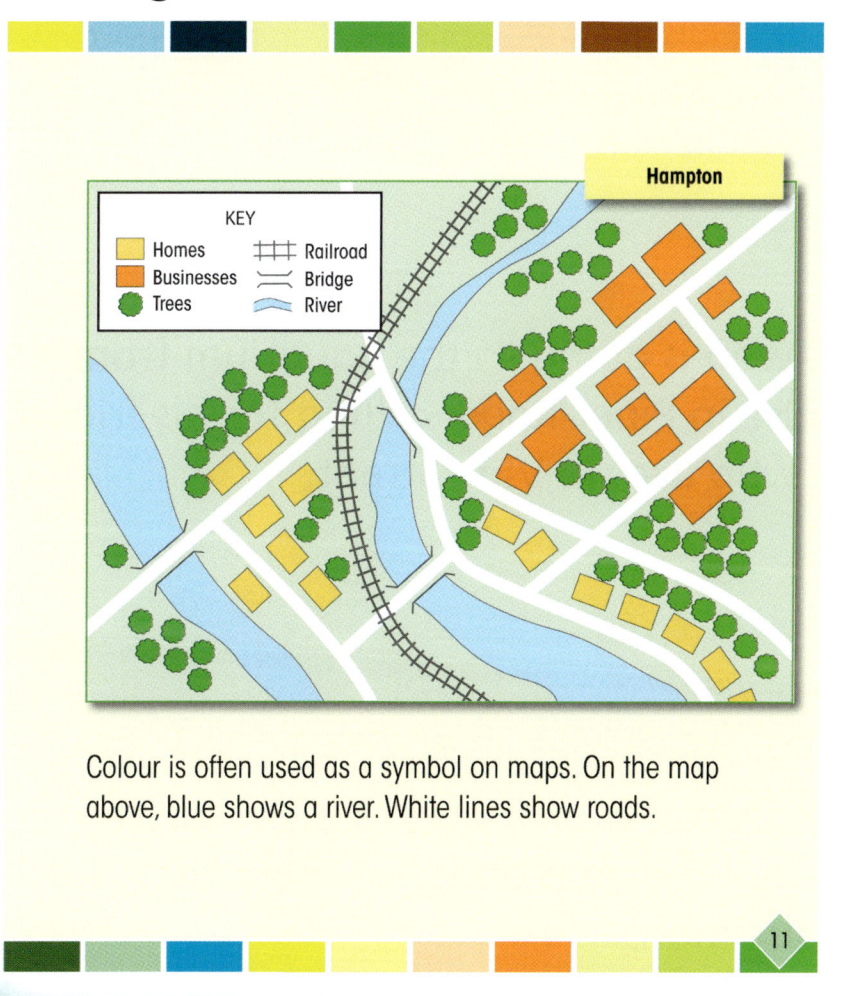

Hampton

KEY
- Homes
- Businesses
- Trees
- Railroad
- Bridge
- River

Colour is often used as a symbol on maps. On the map above, blue shows a river. White lines show roads.

Draw a simple plan of your route from home to school. Use coloured symbols and a key to show the different buildings you pass.

Describe to your friend how to get from school to your house.

Learner Profile Attributes: Thinkers, Well-balanced

Where We Are in Place and Time

Giving directions

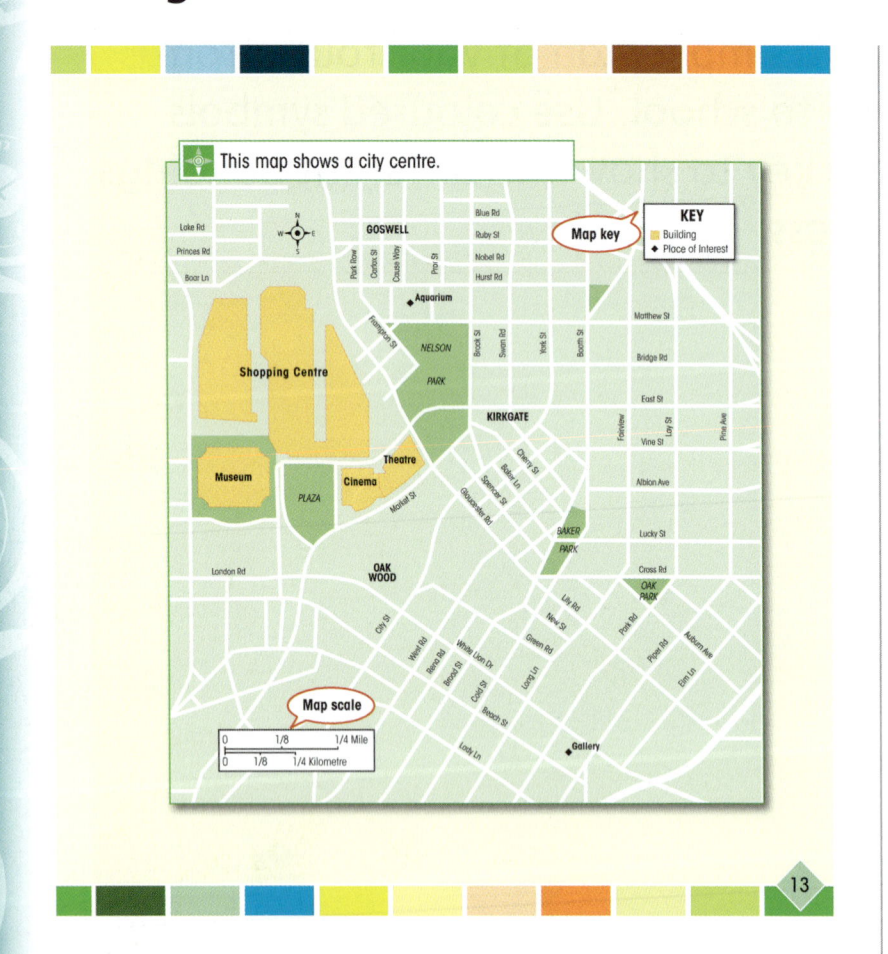

This map shows a city centre.

Look at the map and find:

Lake Road, the cinema, Piper Road, the aquarium, Vine Street

Write directions for:

Sara, who is going to the cinema from her house in Lake Road.

_____

_____

_____

Jason, who is going to the aquarium from his house in Piper Road, calling for his friend Flavio who lives in Vine Street.

_____

_____

_____

Now ask your friend to pick a place from the map and give them the directions.

Learner Profile Attributes: Thinkers, Well-balanced

Where We Are in Place and Time

Planning routes

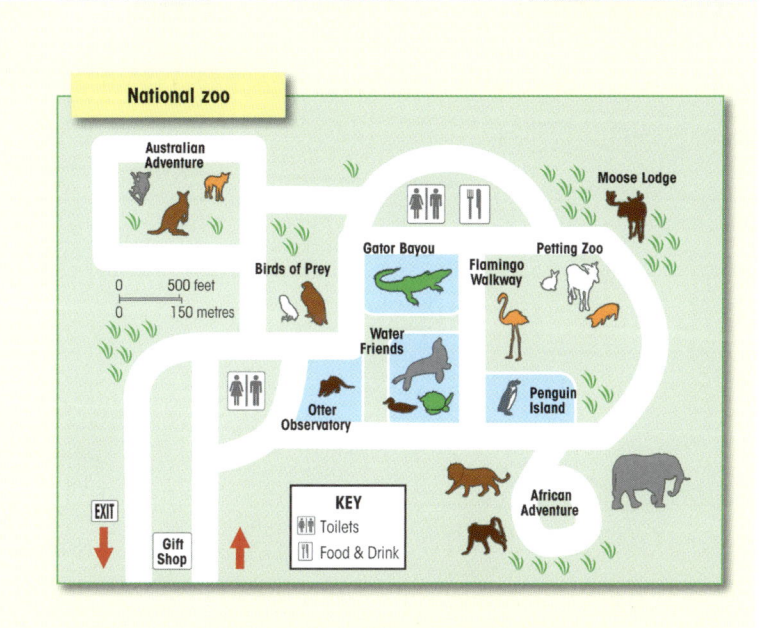

Look at the map of the National zoo and find the scale. The scale lets you work out how big the zoo really is.

Other maps show smaller areas, such as cities or neighbourhoods. They may just show one place, such as a museum or zoo. These maps show more detail than country maps. They may show streets, parks, and important buildings in the area.

On the next page make a plan for your class to do a walking tour of the zoo.

Divide your class into two groups.

The groups must be in different places at different times.

Each group will visit the ten animal areas. Each area takes 15 minutes: ten minutes to walk there and five minutes to watch.

They also need to have lunch (15 minutes) and visit the toilets (15 minutes).

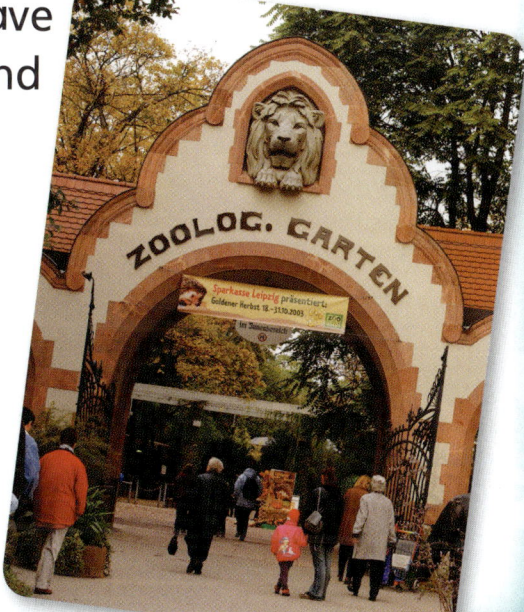

Learner Profile Attributes: Thinkers, Well-balanced

Where We Are in Place and Time

My class zoo visit plan

Time	Group 1	Group 2
10.00		
10.15		
10.30		
10.45		
11.00		
11.15		
11.30		
11.45		
12.00		
12.15		
12.30		
12.45		
13.00	Meet at Gift Shop to go back to school.	Meet at Gift Shop to go back to school.

Learner Profile Attributes: Thinkers, Well-balanced

How We Express Ourselves

Communicating

Secrets

By looking at the picture, what sort of superhero do you think Rick Champion is? What kinds of things might he do?

_____
_____
_____

Rick kept his superhero powers secret. Why do you think he did this?

_____
_____
_____

CHAPTER ONE
BECOMING FEEBLEMAN

Rick Champion was the best footballer Wincey Village Primary had ever seen. He was the top scorer in the school team, and everyone loved him. But Rick had a terrible secret. Rick Champion was a superhero.

Now, most people would give anything to be a superhero. After all, superheroes can run faster than a speeding train, or leap tall buildings in one bound, or save the world before breakfast.
And sometimes all three at once. But Rick Champion wasn't that sort of superhero.

Write some things you are good at that you think others do not know about.

_____
_____
_____

Try to find out something new about one of your friends, for example, a new hobby, or their favourite ice cream flavour!

Learner Profile Attributes: Communicators, Open-minded

How We Express Ourselves

A cartoon strip

Draw a cartoon strip story about one of Feebleman's adventures.

Learner Profile Attributes: Communicators, Open-minded

How We Express Ourselves

Heroes

What is the difference between being famous and being a hero?

Being famous means:

_____

_____

_____

Being a hero means:

_____

_____

_____

Who are some of your real life heroes? Why? Fill in the table below.

Who is my hero?	Why?

Learner Profile Attributes: Communicators, Open-minded

How We Express Ourselves

Who is a hero?

Carry out a survey to see what ten people in your class think about heroes. Add your own heroes and heroines to the list.

Write a tick or a cross for yes or no.

Do you think these people are heroes?										
Nelson Mandela										
Queen Elizabeth II										
Mother Theresa										
Barack Obama										

Did people agree about who is a hero and who is not?

Which famous person did most people choose as a hero? Why do you think this is?

Learner Profile Attributes: Communicators, Open-minded

How We Express Ourselves

Polite greetings

Saying hello

How do you say hello? In some countries it is polite to bow. In other countries people shake hands. What is polite in one place might be rude in another!

In India people say hello with their hands. They put their palms together. Their fingers point up. They may also say *namaste*. This means "I bow to you". Sometimes they greet an **elder** in a special way. An elder is a respected older family member. A younger person sometimes kneels on the ground and touches the elder's feet.

In Tanzania, touching feet means respect, too. People greet elders with the word *shikamoo*. This means "I hold your feet". It is another way to say "I respect you".

The Maori live in New Zealand. They greet each other by pressing their noses together. This greeting is called a *hongi*. They may also say *kia ora*. This means "hello".

▼ Maori greet each other by touching noses.

elder respected older family member
hongi greeting in which two people press their noses together

Look at the information on the right.

How do people greet each other in:

India	
Tanzania	
New Zealand	

How do you say 'hello' to:

your best friend	
your teacher	
your baby sister	

Learner Profile Attributes: Communicators, Open-minded

25

How We Express Ourselves

Polite greetings around the world

There are different ways of greeting people politely in different parts of the world.

---

placing palms of hands together

touching feet   kneeling

rubbing noses   shaking hands

bowing   kissing cheeks

standing when someone enters the room

hugging   giving flowers

leaving shoes at the door

Put a ring around those you have used.

Draw a line under the greetings you have never used.

In Vietnam people greet each other by shaking hands or bowing.

Handshakes and hugs

In Vietnam, people often say hello with a small bow. Sometimes they shake hands. In Brazil, friends hug when they meet. Sometimes they kiss each other's cheeks.

Why do people hug in some countries and bow in others? It is partly because they need different amounts of **personal space**. Your personal space is like a bubble around your body. If someone steps inside it, you feel uneasy.

Personal space needs change from country to country. People in Japan might stand more than 90 centimetres (3 feet) apart when they talk. In Egypt people might stand only 25 centimetres (10 inches) apart.

A person who stands too close may seem rude. But he or she may just be from a country where they need less personal space.

Try it! Talk to a friend. Slowly move closer. When you get too close, does your friend back up? This shows how much personal space your friend needs.

personal space amount of space people need around them to feel comfortable

Which types of greeting do you prefer? Why?

_____

_____

Which types of greeting do you like least? Why?

_____

_____

Learner Profile Attributes: Communicators, Open-minded

How We Express Ourselves

Eating manners

When you eat, do you use your hands, cutlery, or both?

List different types of food and write what you use to eat them with. Ask some friends what they use.

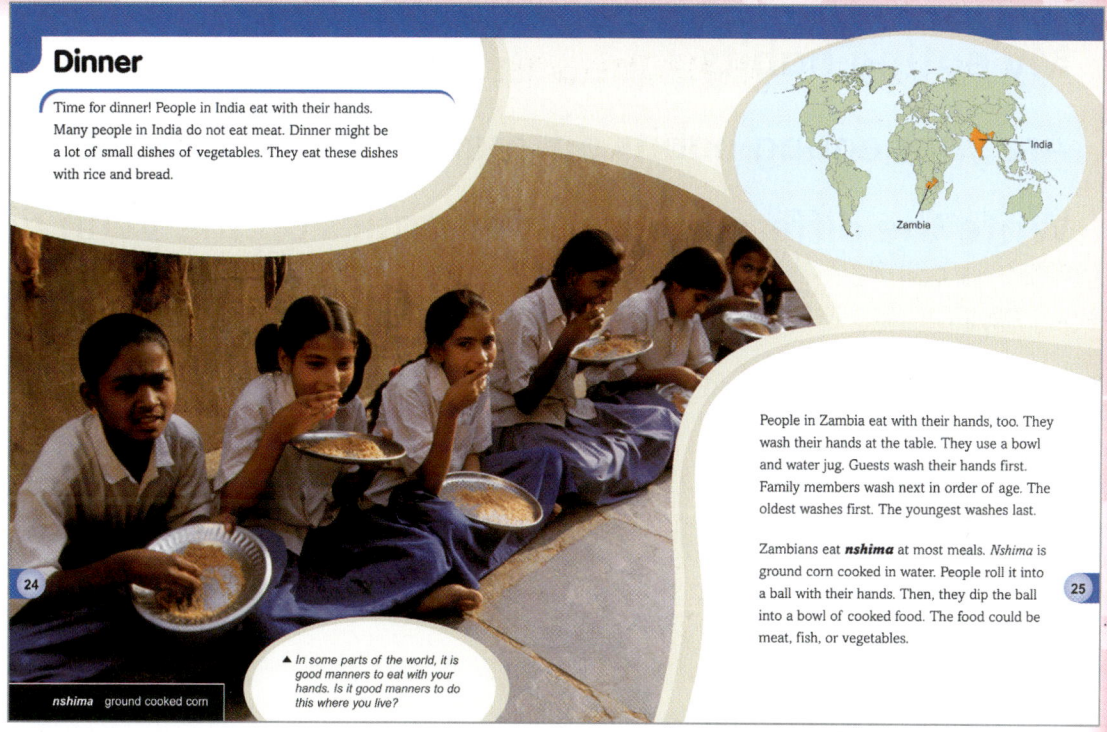

Dinner

Time for dinner! People in India eat with their hands. Many people in India do not eat meat. Dinner might be a lot of small dishes of vegetables. They eat these dishes with rice and bread.

People in Zambia eat with their hands, too. They wash their hands at the table. They use a bowl and water jug. Guests wash their hands first. Family members wash next in order of age. The oldest washes first. The youngest washes last.

Zambians eat **nshima** at most meals. *Nshima* is ground corn cooked in water. People roll it into a ball with their hands. Then, they dip the ball into a bowl of cooked food. The food could be meat, fish, or vegetables.

nshima ground cooked corn

▲ In some parts of the world, it is good manners to eat with your hands. Is it good manners to do this where you live?

hands   knife   fork   spoon   chopsticks

Food	Me	Friend 1	Friend 2

Learner Profile Attributes: Communicators, Open-minded

How We Express Ourselves

My eating habits

Are your eating habits different when you are at home from when you are at school?

Write the differences and similarities on the Venn diagram.

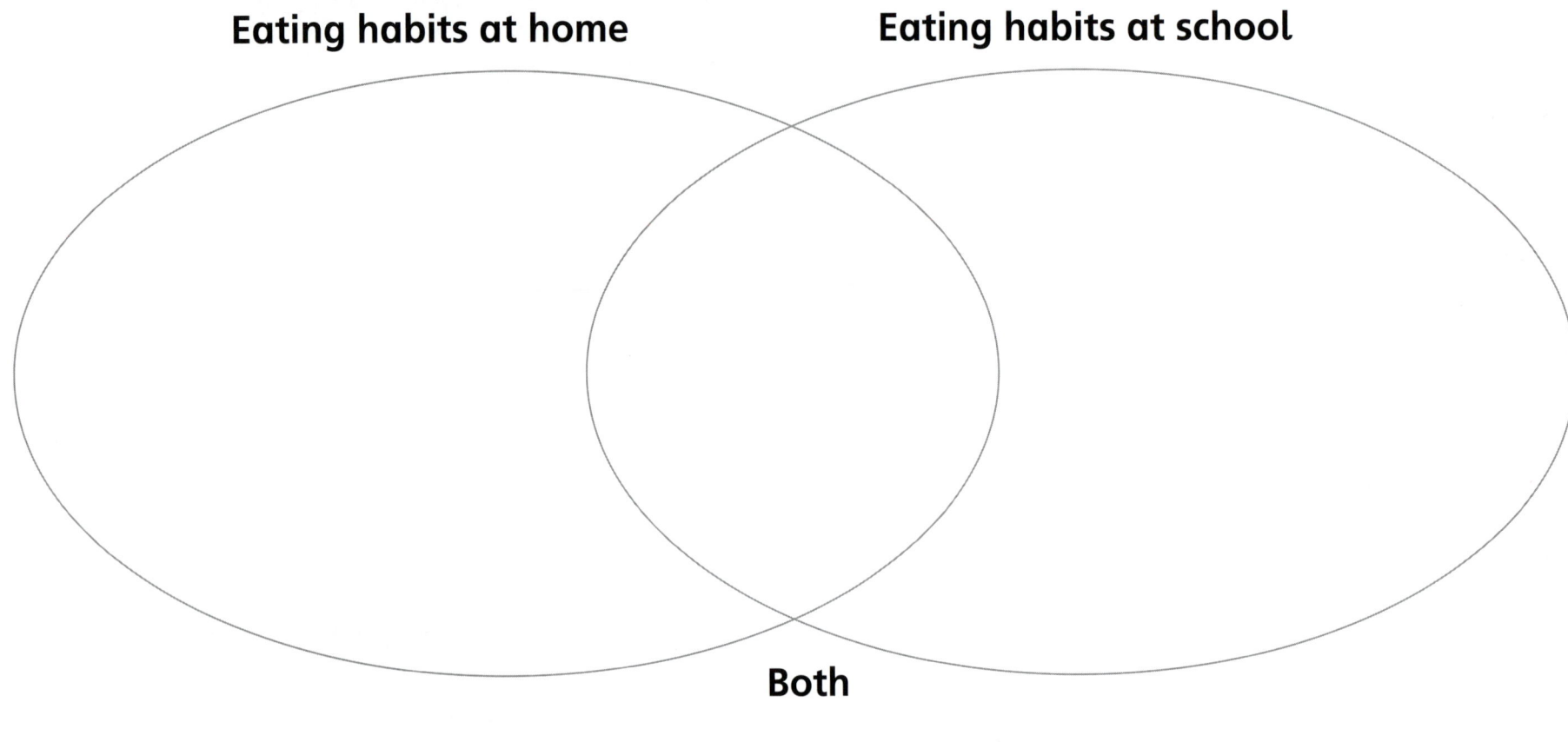

Eating habits at home   **Eating habits at school**

Both

Where do you normally eat your meals? Who with? _____

Does your family have a special way of starting a meal? _____

Learner Profile Attributes: Communicators, Open-minded

How We Express Ourselves

Body language

You may not realise this, but we communicate a lot without words – using our faces, eyes, hands and shoulders.

Body gestures may have different meanings depending on where you are from. What does this body language mean where you live?

shrugging shoulders

_____

raising eyebrows

_____

nodding head

_____

shaking head

_____

holding hand up, palm facing forward

_____

moving and bending index finger

_____

Learner Profile Attributes: Communicators, Open-minded

How We Express Ourselves

Facial expressions

Draw some facial expressions to communicate these meanings.

I'm very excited!　　　I'm not sure…　　　I'm bored.　　　Please don't tell the others!

Now make up your own facial expression puzzles for your friends to guess.

Learner Profile Attributes: Communicators, Open-minded

How the World Works

Water

Where we find water

Take a 'Water Walk' around your house, your school or your community.

Write or draw some of the places where you can find water.

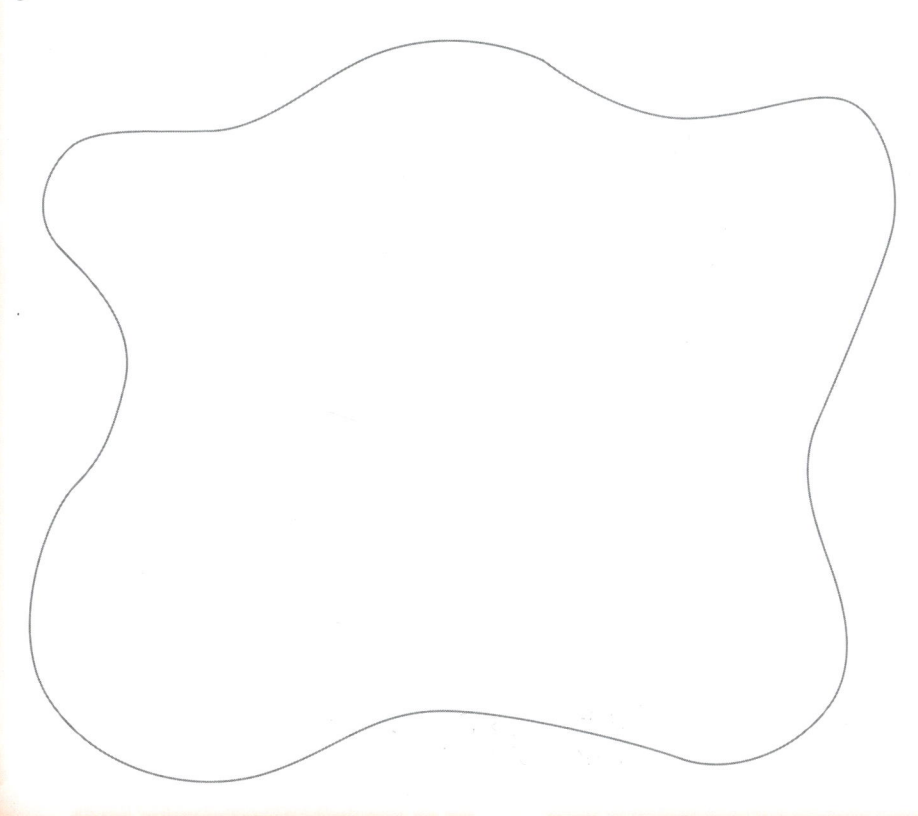

Try to complete this Water Words Alphabet by writing down words to do with water into the grid below.

Water Words Alphabet	A:	B:
C:	D:	E:
F:	G:	H:
I:	J:	K:
L:	M:	N:
O:	P:	Q:
R:	S:	T:
U:	V:	W:
X:	Y:	Z:

Learner Profile Attributes: Caring, Risk-takers

How the World Works

Water words

Look at these words.

> spring   stream   sea   ocean   river
> puddle   lagoon   lake   fountain   brook
> creek   canal   well   pond

Find out what each of these words means.

Put a ring around the words that are areas containing salt water.

Underline the words that are areas containing fresh water.

Using books and atlases, write down some names of:

lakes	rivers
seas	oceans

Put a ring around those that are nearest to you.

Underline those that you have visited.

Learner Profile Attributes: Caring, Risk-takers

How the World Works

Water transport

One morning Brave Mouse was walking by the water when he made a wonderful discovery. A beautiful sailing boat had been washed up on the shore.

It was red with white sails, like seagull wings. Beside the mast was a little wheel. Brave Mouse gazed at the boat and his heart did a little dance.

Carefully, he folded the sails and moved the boat to a safe place. Then he went home and called for his wife and son. "I have great news," said Brave Mouse. "I am going to sail round the world."

In this story, Brave Mouse plans to travel round the world in a sailing boat.

What other types of water transport do you know?

Write each type on a card. Draw or find a picture to stick on the card.
Working with a friend, group the cards in different categories, for example: fast/slow, cheap/expensive, those you have/have not used, noisy/quiet, on top of/in the water.

Learner Profile Attributes: Caring, Risk-takers

33

How the World Works

Seas and oceans

Using an atlas to help you, list the seas and oceans you would cross to sail round the world from where you live.

_____

_____

_____

_____

_____

Find out which sea or ocean is:

1. the widest: _____

2. the deepest: _____

3. the saltiest: _____

4. the coldest: _____

Write your own version of an adventure story based on the places you have listed.

Learner Profile Attributes: Caring, Risk-takers

How the World Works

Changing water

Changing water

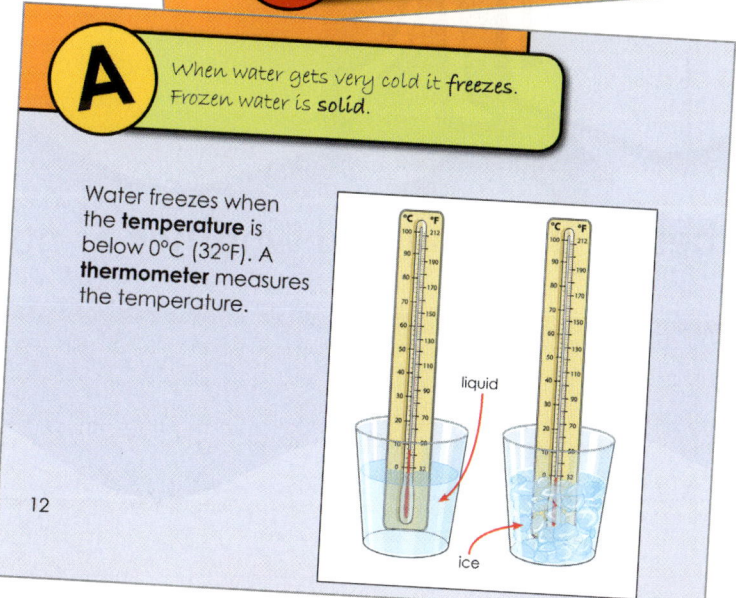

Most of the water in the ocean is **liquid**. The water we drink and wash with is liquid. Rainwater is liquid.

Q: What happens when water gets very cold?

A: When water gets very cold it **freezes**. Frozen water is **solid**.

Water freezes when the **temperature** is below 0°C (32°F). A **thermometer** measures the temperature.

Where have you seen solid water (ice)?

Draw some examples.

What happens when ice gets warm?

_____

_____

_____

_____

Learner Profile Attributes: Caring, Risk-takers

How the World Works

Ice cube experiment

Try this experiment.

Put two ice cubes on two flat dishes. Put one dish in the sun and one in the fridge.

Look at them every 15 minutes. Record on the table below the time and whether or not the cubes are solid, liquid or gas.

Time	Start:				
ice cube 1 (sun)	solid				
ice cube 2 (fridge)	solid				

Learner Profile Attributes: Caring, Risk-takers

How the World Works

Measuring water

Look around your home and see how many different containers you can find for holding water. Draw some of them here.

Draw lines to match the containers that you think can hold the same amount.

Put a ring around the container you think can hold the most water.

Put a tick next to the container you think can hold the least water.

> Some countries measure water in litres and millilitres (this is called the metric system). Some countries measure water in pints and gallons (called the imperial system).
>
> Which system do you use? _____

Learner Profile Attributes: Caring, Risk-takers

How the World Works

Experiments with containers

Experiment 1

Choose two containers that you think have the same capacity.

Fill one container with water.

Pour the water into the second container.

Was your estimation right? Did both containers hold the same amount of water? Was the second container too big, too small or just right?

Experiment 2

Choose six containers and put them in order from highest to lowest capacity. Record your prediction.

Prediction						
Results (ml)						

Now compare the capacity of different pairs of containers to check your order. Record your results.

If you make a mess working with water, remember to clear it up!

Experiment 3

You can measure how quickly water flows. We write this as litres per second.

Choose a tap. Working with a partner and using a stop watch, time how long it takes to fill a 1 litre bottle.

Record your results. Try again with different taps. Which tap is the quickest?

Learner Profile Attributes: Caring, Risk-takers

How the World Works

Water for life

Water for life

Plants, animals, and people are living things. All living things need water to live.

4

People need to drink about 8 glasses of water a day.

More than half your body is water. People need to drink water to stay healthy. People also need water to wash themselves and to grow plants for food.

5

Make a list of the ways that you use water.

Compare your list with a friend's list.

Choose some things that are on both lists and record how much water you use each day.

What water is used for:	Me	Friend
drinking		
cleaning teeth		

Water is precious and many people live with very little water.

On a new piece of paper, make a poster to help people to save water.

Learner Profile Attributes: Caring, Risk-takers

39

How the World Works

Where does our water come from?

People can also get water from under the ground. Many people get their water from underground wells. Other people get their water from rivers and lakes. The water travels through pipes to taps in people's houses.

The water we use has travelled a long way. It has gone from bodies of water to clouds and back again as rain. Trees, plants, and animals can only live on Earth because of water. Water is very important in our lives so we must not waste a tiny drop.

29

Draw a diagram to show how water gets to your taps.

Show as many different stages as you can.

Learner Profile Attributes: Caring, Risk-takers

40

How We Organise Ourselves

Weather and Seasons

The water cycle

Changing weather

The Sun, air, and water cause changes in the weather. The Sun warms Earth and this moves air and water around. This is known as the water cycle.

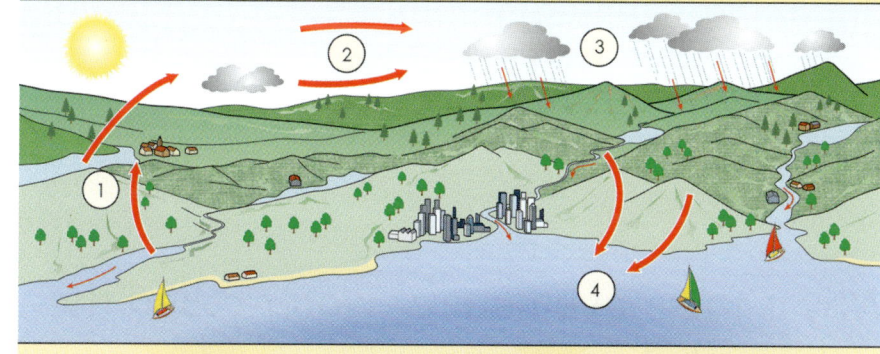

1. The Sun's heat evaporates water from sea and living things.
2. Water vapour rises and cools to form clouds.
3. Clouds are blown by the wind. They contain tiny drops of water that fall as rain or snow.
4. Water soaks into the ground or flows into rivers and lakes on its way to the sea.

Look at the picture of the water cycle on the left.

Use your own words to describe each stage.

1. _____

2. _____

3. _____

4. _____

Learner Profile Attributes: Knowledgeable, Thinkers

How We Organise Ourselves

Water and other natural cycles

Here are some words that describe what happens in a water cycle.

Evaporation is when water gets warm and turns into vapour.

Condensation is when water vapour cools and turns into liquid.

Draw some examples of evaporation.

Draw some examples of condensation.

What other natural cycles do you know?

_____
_____
_____
_____

What does the word cycle mean?

_____
_____
_____

Why is the movement of water called the water cycle?

_____
_____
_____

Learner Profile Attributes: Knowledgeable, Thinkers

How We Organise Ourselves

Seasons

A year is divided into different periods, each with a different kind of weather. Each of these periods is called a season.

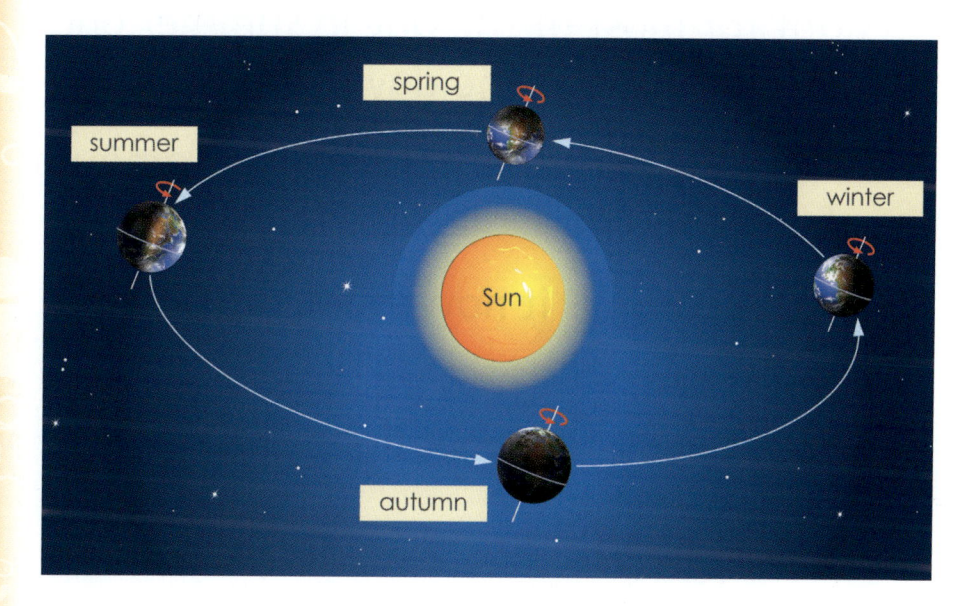

Look at the picture. Some parts of the world have four seasons.

Write them in order:

| 1. S_____ | 2. S_____ |
| 3. A_____ | 4. W_____ |

Some parts of the world have only two seasons.

In the place where you live, how many seasons do you have? Which are they?

_____
_____
_____

On a big sheet of paper draw what happens in the different seasons.

Divide your paper for two or four seasons, depending on where you live.

Learner Profile Attributes: Knowledgeable, Thinkers

How We Organise Ourselves

Hot or cold, light or dark?

Look at the map.

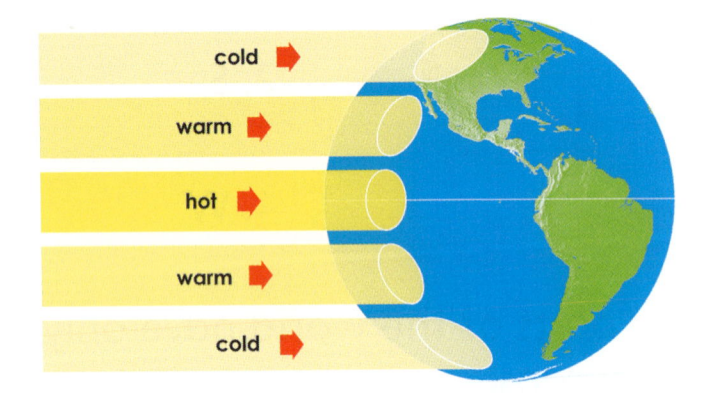

The hottest part of Earth is a band around the middle called the Equator. Mark the Equator on the map.

The coldest parts of Earth are the North and South Poles. Mark the North Pole and the South Pole on the map.

Where do you live? Is it in a cold, warm or hot part of the world?

_____

In some parts of the world there is more daylight in some seasons and less in others.

At the North and South Poles it can be light for most of the day in summer and dark for most of the day in winter.

At the Equator there is the same amount of light and dark all year round.

What season is it now where you live?

_____

What time does it get light and dark?

It gets light at _____

It gets dark at _____

What time do you go to bed?

_____

Is it normally still light when you go to bed? _____

Learner Profile Attributes: Knowledgeable, Thinkers

How We Organise Ourselves

Measuring weather

A **temperature** shows how hot or cold something is. This chart shows the temperature during a year in one part of the world.

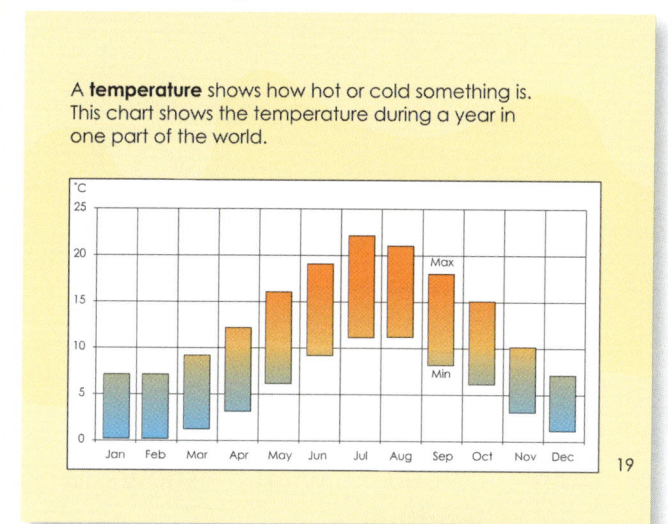

19

It shows how much rain has fallen. This device is called a **rain gauge**.

Scientists at weather stations measure how much rain falls every month. They also measure **temperature** and wind speed.

26

Look at the pictures of these measuring instruments. What can we measure with these things?

| rainfall | wind direction | temperature | wind speed |

A thermometer measures

A rain gauge measures

An anemometer measures

A weather vane measures

Learner Profile Attributes: Knowledgeable, Thinkers

45

How We Organise Ourselves

Predicting the weather

Measuring weather helps us to predict what the weather will be like.

Why is this important?

_____

_____

Keep a weather chart for two weeks.

Make a list of the different kinds of weather you might have. Create your own symbols to use in your chart.

Mon	Tue	Wed	Thu	Fri	Sat	Sun

Mon	Tue	Wed	Thu	Fri	Sat	Sun

Draw a graph from your results.

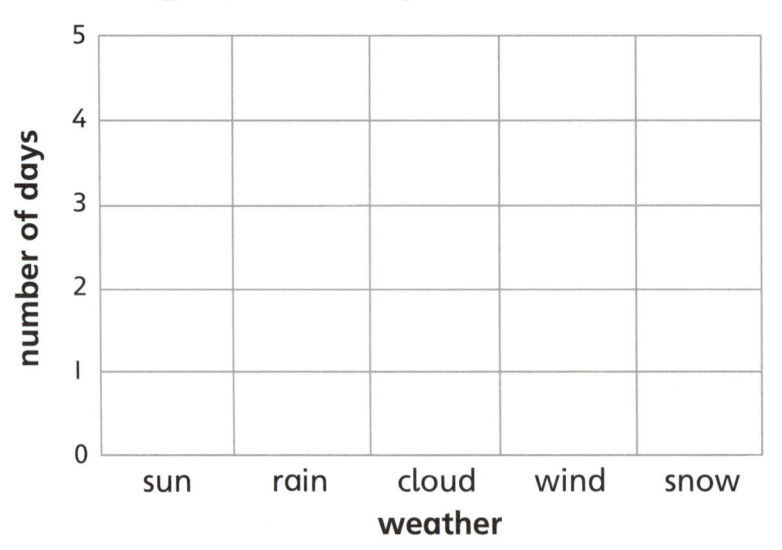

(graph: y-axis "number of days" 0–5; x-axis "weather": sun, rain, cloud, wind, snow)

Write some conclusions from your graph.

_____

_____

_____

What kind of weather did you have most in the past two weeks?

_____

What do you predict the weather will be like next week? _____

Learner Profile Attributes: Knowledgeable, Thinkers

How We Organise Ourselves

Extreme weather

It is useful to know about dangerous weather. Big storms and strong winds can damage buildings and trees. By watching the weather carefully, scientists can guess how weather will change. They can warn us to be ready for bad weather.

27

The changing weather and **seasons** are important for all living things. Rain helps plants grow but too much rain can kill plants. The weather can bring blue skies or beautiful rainbows. It can also bring strong winds, storms, and floods.

28

↑ Floods are caused by too much rain. The water can wash away soil and knock buildings down.

Look at the pictures.

List some kinds of weather that can be dangerous.

Pretend you are a newspaper reporter. Choose a type of weather from your list. Write a story about someone caught in dangerous weather.

Learner Profile Attributes: Knowledgeable, Thinkers

47

How We Organise Ourselves

Extreme weather problems

Collect extreme weather stories and pictures from newspapers and magazines.

Make a list of some of the problems extreme weather can cause.

too hot	too cold	too much rain	no rain	too much wind	too much snow

Mark on a map in your classroom where these problems happened.

Carry out a survey to find out whether people in your school have ever been affected by different kinds of extreme weather.

Learner Profile Attributes: Knowledgeable, Thinkers

How We Organise Ourselves

How weather affects our lives

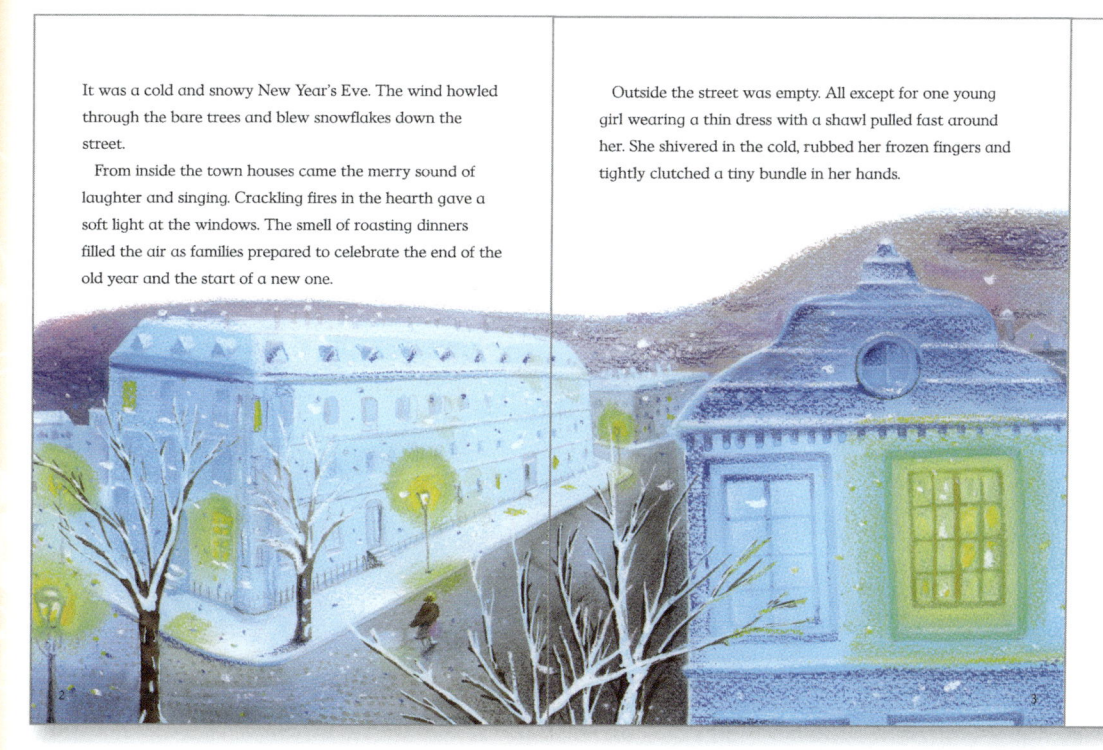

It was a cold and snowy New Year's Eve. The wind howled through the bare trees and blew snowflakes down the street.

From inside the town houses came the merry sound of laughter and singing. Crackling fires in the hearth gave a soft light at the windows. The smell of roasting dinners filled the air as families prepared to celebrate the end of the old year and the start of a new one.

Outside the street was empty. All except for one young girl wearing a thin dress with a shawl pulled fast around her. She shivered in the cold, rubbed her frozen fingers and tightly clutched a tiny bundle in her hands.

In the cold dawn of New Year's Day a child lay in a doorway. Her eyes were shut and her hair hung lifeless around her pale cheeks, but her lips were frozen in the most beautiful smile.

The ground by her feet was littered with black, spent matchsticks.

"Poor little thing!" cried the townspeople when they found her body. "She was just trying to keep herself warm!"

This is the beginning and end of the story of *Little Match Girl*. Write the rest of the story. Why was she outside on a cold winter night?

Learner Profile Attributes: Knowledgeable, Thinkers

49

How We Organise Ourselves

How weather and seasons affect our lives

Changes in weather and seasons affect our lives in many ways.

What seasons are there where you live? Divide the white area into as many columns as you need (one column for each season). Write the name of the seasons as the column titles, then write how the seasonal weather affects what you eat, the clothes you wear, the things you do and how you feel.

	Seasons
What I eat	
The clothes I wear	
The things I do	
How I feel	

Learner Profile Attributes: Knowledgeable, Thinkers

Sharing the Planet

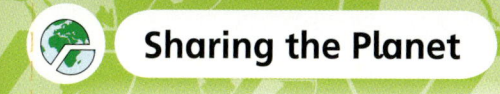

Disappearing Forests

The last tree

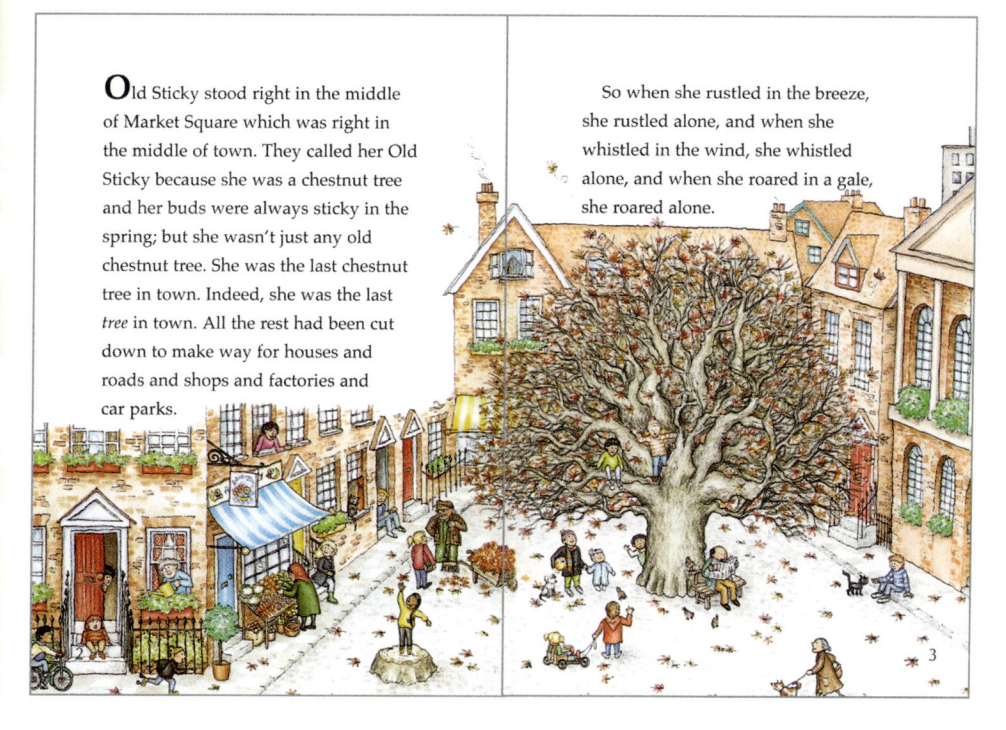

Old Sticky stood right in the middle of Market Square which was right in the middle of town. They called her Old Sticky because she was a chestnut tree and her buds were always sticky in the spring; but she wasn't just any old chestnut tree. She was the last chestnut tree in town. Indeed, she was the last *tree* in town. All the rest had been cut down to make way for houses and roads and shops and factories and car parks.

So when she rustled in the breeze, she rustled alone, and when she whistled in the wind, she whistled alone, and when she roared in a gale, she roared alone.

How do you feel when you read the start of this story?

What do you think will happen next?

All the other trees in the story have been cut down.

When a tree is cut down, what can we use it for?

_____

_____

_____

_____

When a tree is still growing, are there any parts of it that we can use?

_____

_____

_____

_____

Learner Profile Attributes: Caring, Principled, Reflective

Sharing the Planet

How do you feel?

But in spite of everything they said, it was decided there and then that Old Sticky had to be cut down, and right away.

Up came the men from the timber-yard with their saws and ladders and ropes. They measured out how high Old Sticky was and tied ropes to her branches. They worked out where she would fall and marked off a danger area. They put on their yellow helmets and sharpened their saws.

Describe the people in the picture.

_____

_____

_____

_____

Imagine you are a man from the timber yard.

How do you feel about cutting down the tree?

Now imagine you are one of the children.

How do you feel about cutting down the tree?

Learner Profile Attributes: Caring, Principled, Reflective

Sharing the Planet

Trees around us

Take a 'Tree Walk'. Count the number of trees in a garden, school playground or on your route to school.

Use tally marks IIII to record them.

Type of tree	Number of trees
Small trees (the trunk is thinner than you)	
Medium trees (you can put your arms around the trunk)	
Big trees (the trunk is too big to get your arms around it)	

Draw a map of the garden, playground or route to show where the trees are.

Learner Profile Attributes: Caring, Principled, Reflective

Sharing the Planet

Grouping trees and leaves

Collect one leaf from each tree (try to take leaves that have already fallen).

Find different ways to sort the leaves into sets, for example: by colour, size, or shape. Draw some of your sets here.

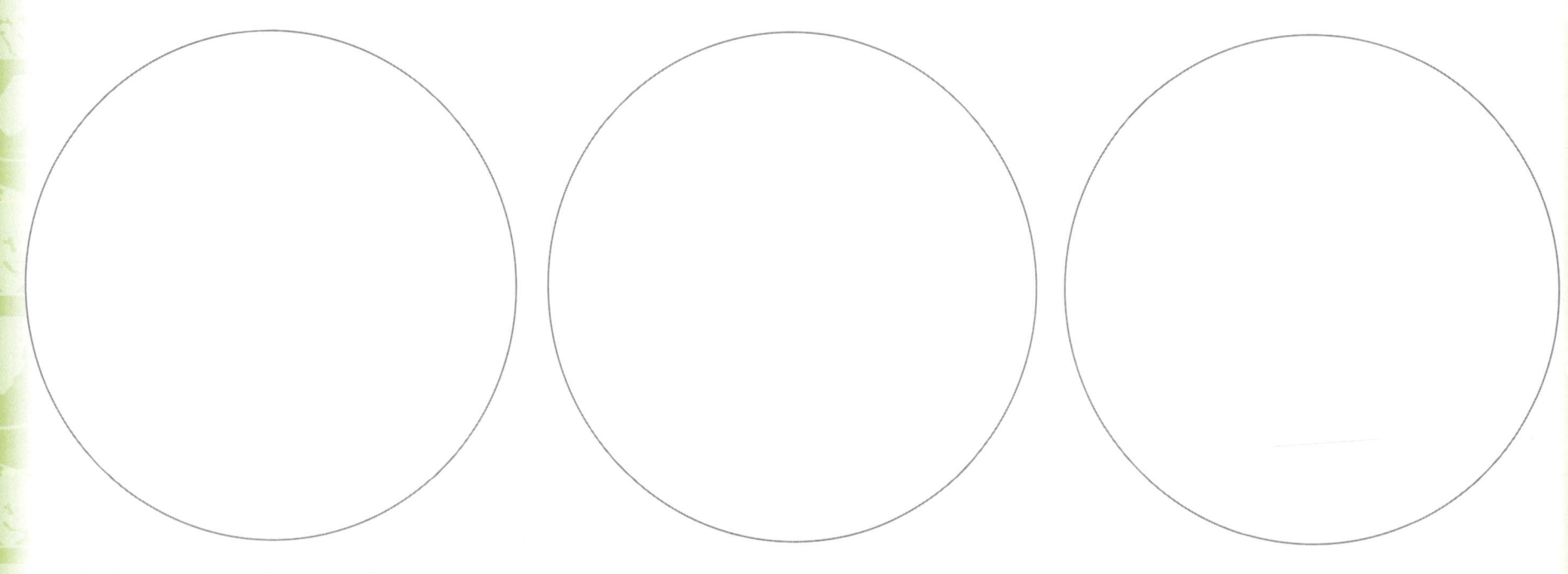

Stick some of your leaves on to a big sheet of card to make a poster.

Try to find out the names of the trees they come from. Write the names on your poster.

Test your friends to see if they know the names of the trees.

Learner Profile Attributes: Caring, Principled, Reflective

Sharing the Planet

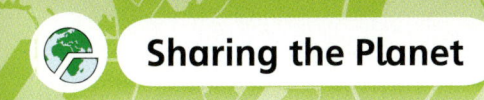

How we use wood

Look around you.
Draw or write all the things you see that are made from wood.

Try to find out what types of wood are used to make these things.

Sharing the Planet

Properties of wood

Why do we use wood for so many things?

Write a list of its properties.

Compare your own list with a friend's list.

Look again at the page where you drew or wrote about all the things that are made from wood.

Make a list of those that could be made from a different material instead of wood.

Item	Alternative material

Learner Profile Attributes: Caring, Principled, Reflective

Sharing the Planet

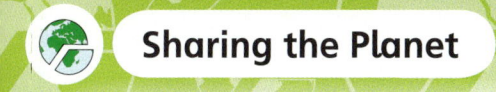

Why are forests disappearing?

Cutting down rainforests

Half the trees on this hillside have been cut down.

People are cutting down millions of trees in rainforests. These people work for companies that are clearing the land for farming. Some companies sell the wood to people in other countries.

Making farmland

People clear parts of the rainforest to grow farm **crops**. Farmers grow just one kind of plant, such as oil palms or rubber trees. All the different kinds of plants that grew there before are destroyed.

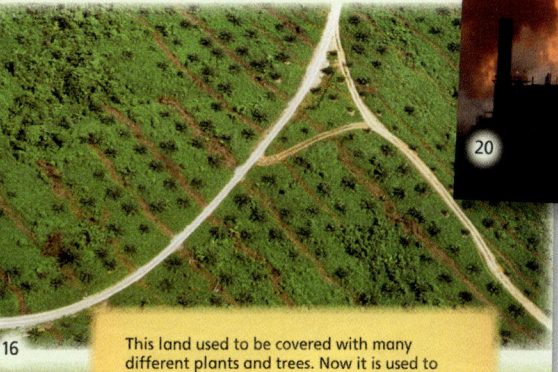

This land used to be covered with many different plants and trees. Now it is used to grow oil palm plants.

Acid rain

Forests are also being damaged by **pollution** from factories and **power stations**. Smoke and gases from factories and power stations escape into the air. The smoke and gases mix into the rain. This is called **acid rain.**

Acid rain kills the leaves of trees. Once the leaves are damaged, the trees die. Some forests are losing many trees because of acid rain.

Most of the trees in this forest have been killed by acid rain.

Look at the pictures. Talk to a friend about what is happening.

Where in the world do you think these pictures were taken?

Look in newspapers and magazines to find other pictures that show how and why forests are disappearing.

Learner Profile Attributes: Caring, Principled, Reflective

Sharing the Planet

Causes and effects

Think about why forests are disappearing (the causes).

Think about what happens after they disappear (the effects).

Write your ideas on the arrows.

Causes   **Effects**

Choose one of these causes and make a poster showing what can be done to stop the problem.

Learner Profile Attributes: Caring, Principled, Reflective

Sharing the Planet

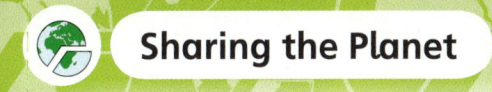

What can we do?

Replacing forests

Fir trees grow much faster than rainforest trees. Young fir trees only take a few years to grow big enough to replace trees that have been cut down.

Check the things you buy that are made from trees. See if they come from sustainable forests.

Some companies always plant new trees to replace fir trees they have cut down. These forests are called **sustainable forests**. People can help to save forests by buying paper and wood from sustainable forests.

💬 What does sustainable mean?

Using books and the Internet, try to find out how old trees are when they are cut down.

Learner Profile Attributes: Caring, Principled, Reflective

Sharing the Planet

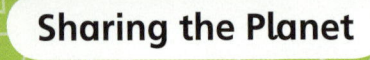

Saving our forests

Saving paper

If people use less paper, fewer trees need to be cut down. One way of saving paper is to reuse old paper, such as wrapping paper.

Recycling one tonne of paper saves 17 trees from being cut down.

Recycling paper also means that fewer trees are cut down. Newspapers, magazines, and cardboard are processed and made into more paper. We can all help to protect the forests by recycling.

29

📖 We can help save forests if we reduce, reuse, recycle. What do these three words mean?

Reduce means:

_____

_____

Reuse means:

_____

_____

Recycle means:

_____

_____

💬 Think of two things you can do to help save forests:

a) at school …
b) at home …

60   Learner Profile Attributes: Caring, Principled, Reflective

Reflection

Overview

Organising theme	Unit title
	|//
Central idea	
Write about one line of inquiry from this unit and say how you investigated it.	Write here some of the questions you asked.

Learner Profile

Write a few lines to show how you used your Learner Profile attributes.

Unit title: _____

I am becoming a good …

Inquirer _____
_____

Thinker _____
_____

Communicator _____
_____

Risk-taker _____
_____

I am trying to become …

Knowledgeable _____

Principled _____

Open-minded _____

Well-balanced _____

Reflective _____

Caring _____

Trans-disciplinary Skills

Highlight the trans-disciplinary skills you used in this unit.

Unit title: _____

Trans-disciplinary Skills

Social Skills

Accepting responsibility
Respecting others
Co-operating
Resolving conflict
Group decision making

Communication Skills

Listening
Speaking
Reading
Writing
Non-verbal communication
Graphic presentation

Thinking Skills

Acquisition of knowledge
Comprehension
Application
Analysis
Synthesis
Evaluation
Dialectical (logical) thought
Metacognition

Research Skills

Formulating questions
Observing
Planning
Collecting data
Recording data
Organising data
Interpreting data
Presenting research findings

Self-management Skills

Gross motor skills
Fine motor skills
Spatial awareness
Organisation
Time management
Safety
Healthy lifestyle
Codes of behaviour
Informed choices

Attitudes

Unit title

Look at these words:

| appreciation | commitment | confidence | co-operation | creativity | curiosity |
| empathy | enthusiasm | independence | integrity | respect | tolerance |

Circle the attitudes this unit has helped you to develop.

Now choose one of the attitudes from the box above. Draw or write about a situation when you demonstrated this attitude.